A Dynamic Exchange
Between Us

ALSO BY ANTHONY CALESHU

POETRY

The Victor Poems
Of Whales: in Print, in Paint, in Sea, in Stars, in Coin, in House, in Margins
The Siege of the Body and a Brief Respite

FICTION

Churchtown: The Tale of Suzy Delou and Faye Fiddle

CRITICISM

In the Air: Essays on the Poetry of Peter Gizzi (Ed.)
Reconfiguring the Modern American Lyric: The Poetry of James Tate
Poetry and Public Language (Ed. with Tony Lopez)

Anthony Caleshu

A Dynamic Exchange Between Us

Shearsman Books

First published in the United Kingdom in 2019 by
Shearsman Books
50 Westons Hill Drive
Emersons Green
BRISTOL
BS16 7DF

Shearsman Books Ltd Registered Office
30–31 St. James Place, Mangotsfield, Bristol BS16 9JB
(this address not for correspondence)

www.shearsman.com

ISBN 978-1-84861-631-8

ACKNOWLEDGEMENTS
Thank you to Philip Coleman and Peter Gizzi for conversations
during the writing of this book.

Thank you to the editors of the following magazines
where poems first appeared, often in different forms:
*Cassandra Voices, Granta, Magma, Mechanic's Institute Review,
Poetry Ireland Review.*

Contents

*

*

*

for Ciara, Parker, Caleb

Wonder – is not precisely Knowing
And not precisely Knowing not –

Emily Dickinson

I am not quite you, but almost, the opposite of visionary.

Frank O'Hara

WITH YOUR PERMISSION, ALLOW ME TO PERFORM EXEMPLARY SURGERY ON YOUR BRAIN

With your permission, allow me to perform exemplary surgery on your brain. The light breaking through your eyes may be lax but it's also enough to see that your ever-ecstatic memory is full of mnemonic enemies. Woeful of rebirth as a donkey or the fly on a donkey's tail, it's impossible to live a productive life of care without circumstance. It may be easy for me to say disregard the whip and long sword, but know that I know the rope-bridge you're standing on burns from both ends. Elbow-deep in your head, the surgeon of your dreams may not be me, prodding your temporal lobe with a virtual pen, but both of us can see there's much to be gained in terms of scintillation and smell. Though we aim to find and reflect all the mystery in the world, it's as hard to possess as it is to predict. A little to the left and one's thoughts of salvation slip into the water to swim with alligators and leeches. Too much to the right and we'll miss landing on the turtle's back, to harmonize with the river that winds like blood through our connected minds.

WE ARE NOT OF THIS WORLD

Consider the dramatic events that become ordinary people like us. We're not feeling exceptionally valued, but well enough. Whoever amongst us is the most apprehensive and, similarly dictatorial, will understand the world by syllogisms: *I am not of the world. You are of the world. I am not you.* There's so much more to say, but let's say it later. For now, let's think about the phonetic, the diagraphic stickiness that comes when someone wants you gone from their world. There's more than a semantic difference between: *I want to spend a lifetime UN-knowing you,* and *Say another word, and I'll blow your brains out!* The word is both a blessing and a warning. I could say I love you – but then I'd have to kill you. You say this with a smile on your face. To those overhearing our conversation: listen closely and they'll hear you saving my life.

YOUR WORDS OF HURT AND HOLINESS

Your words of hurt and holiness stretch me into an ever-expanding mode of interiority. Over here, there's a projective experience to be had, a predicative mode of me drinking inside of me, even when I'm feeling outside my milieu, outside your window, outside this lake, which reflects the depth of the moon, the depth of all of our shadow-ness. Nightly I stand naked in the shadows, trying to understand the paradox that when drunk I can't remember what I can't forget when sober... making me leave this lake for the Waffle House. At the crossroads of life and death, this bellwether for the State of Emergency stays open, reminding us there's damage worse elsewhere. What I'm feeling right now, when the waffles are flowing in the right direction, is a shamanic, discursive, omnipotence that comes from believing I'm right about at least one thing in this world – whoever you are / whoever I am – this is a deictic moment in delineated time and amorphous space. Feeling morphs into new feeling, requiring me to barf up the moon, barf up the lake, barf up the waffles with a logic that's both fixed and denied, that turns my bones to batter, that makes my bones break.

BECAUSE I AM TO YOU A MESSENGER WORTHY OF ALL TRUST…

trust me to send this lukewarm chowder back to the kitchen. This think-tank we're in believes the world nigh, and yet we've just released data concerning the beginning of time. Allow me this moment to be dubious: Is this a date? Are you trying to kill me? Are you trying to kiss me? The pillow you carry in your handbag is packed with lipstick and punches. And now that you're punching me, really punching me, our place in the world is finally coming into focus. Our grappling under the table leads me to invite you back to my apartment – pigments interspersed at the tops of trees, the roofs of our heads camouflaged in the clouds. Though the valet points our way home, the threat of a cop with a breathalyser means we should take a cab. But we were only having mint tea. And I am only a cousin of the Maharaja. And you are only a cousin of the Maharani.

THE CREATURELY AMONGST US
ARE CELEBRATING THE ADVENT
OF A VANQUISHED SPECIES

The creaturely amongst us are celebrating the advent of a vanquished species. It takes the fallen to know the fallen, say the fallen. In the desert, or alone at sea, all living things know no word can overcome another word – not *belief*, neither *doubt*. Our confessions about loneliness and congregation are the stuff of devotion: who sent me here (this island)? who called me here (the sky)? we ask ourselves daily. If there's a God within us, there's a God outside us: equal and opposite, and so on, and so on. We wander and return, getting lost in the spirit world, now rent but thick with so many of our kind. We reconstitute the wilderness within us constantly. From the backs of our throats, pooling up from the lungs, we sweat abjection until spontaneous-combustion. We make our way by the light in our bodies: shining out of every eye, every pore.

THERE IS MASS CONFUSION
ON THE HIGHWAY

There is mass confusion on the highway: gridlock, pile-ups, cars over-turned. On the outskirts of town, the wind whips the wrappers off cheeseburgers to swirl in a tornado. People flee what they know, as readily as what they don't, so we have the usual complications that come with proclamations of divinity. The way we once did business, trading life for death and death for life, correlated with a byzantine mode of bartering – swine for souls and souls for swine. Some of us became fearful, some of us nonchalant. But now we are moving again, *en route* to being borne again. We see clearly by the headlights of our SUVs, the lost and the dead wandering readily along the roadside. A shepherd in a wide-brim hat stops us from rubber-necking and, with a tired wave of the hand, directs us from one lane into the next.

THE WOLVES EMBROIDERED
ON THIS EPHOD…

won't stop their howling. There's a fidelity between my howl and your heart which is appropriately counter-intuitive. The relationship between our atonement for sin and our devotion to one another is bathed in the blood of the sacrificed, now spattered on our ephods – *red to the blue, to the gold of the blue, to the red!* we cheer from the grandstands. The wolves are twined with bells and pomegranates and studded in the diamantes and emeralds that mean mo' money = mo' life. Our ephods may look like we're dressed to kill, but inside we're as soft as the bunnies that had to die to make our eye-lashes thicker. Wolves that we are and wolves that we become need no agency to sanctify this altar. To worship one another, we agree, is to fall like a leaf in this tabernacle of fallen leaves.

I AM ALL *I KNOW YOU* AGAIN

And because I am all *I know you*, all bets are off. The bet that, like a new God, you have eyes in the back of your head. The bet that, like an old God, you will love me forever. We both hope the octopus we saw yesterday in the aquarium will live, even though most die less than a week after giving birth. Now you are all, how can I *be* again? And because you are all how can I *be?*, the sun is setting over the beach where we are eating pizza. The pizza delivery guy has stayed and we're wondering what we would have done without him. Not just because we don't have a car, but because he's a really cool guy who also works part time at the aquarium and so knows that the most beautiful thing we can experience is the very awe which is impenetrable to us. This knowledge, this *feeling*, he says, is at the centre of true religiousness, which is at the centre of every poetic tragedy. But this is no poem – nor tragedy – it happens, so we're told, to every octopus giving birth anywhere in the world.

I AM NOT WORTHY OF THE LEAST
OF ALL MERCIES

And because I am not worthy of the least of all mercies, I can sense someone taking me by the shoulder, kissing my head, playfully batting my eye. The midnight sun appears when the clouds disperse to the hoots of owls and my memory of charging a bikini wax to the company before opening night. An Italian ice was later bought for me by the nicest guy, who taught me there's no reason not to spend it like you're gonna lose it, *anyway*. Because, *anyway*… All good things are eventually punctuated in this city by scaffolding going up or coming down: clanging poles and heavy joints dropped to shatter the transparency of wind-shields. A stretch of stained-glass from the worshipful house across the street bleeds blue light at our feet. The last thing you should ever do, I was once told before being torn asunder, is interrupt the reverie – unless you're the reverie.

A DYNAMIC EXCHANGE BETWEEN US

A dynamic exchange is happening between us. We could surf pure existence on the back of our Likes, or just skip it for a pop-up party on Facebook at a house that looks just like yours in the suburbs. All my life, I'd been hoping for a religious experience starring you as the silhouette next door, but now we're both unframed and window-less and streaking naked across the front lawn. Inside us, there's a spark that sets alight the topiary that's been clipped in the shape of our genitalia. To the police we explain life and death is happening all around, incoming but similarly external, which is why we burn when we pee on the peeing garden statue. My beer is my beer, one gate-crasher says to another, which leads to another gate-crasher crashing through the front gate. We're just trying to satisfy the regulative ideal that comes when the fire in our soul rages beyond the water games spouted from the nipples of nymphs. This loftiness of being is beyond *beyond*. Verily, verily, someone shouts out an upstairs window. In your parents' bedroom, a pair of legs is opening like language.

BECAUSE I AM THIRSTY

Because I am thirsty I need to drink before I can continue *blowing your mind.* The knowledge you once had about your own imagination required an alarm system with a direct line to the police. The peach you're eating is so sweet, no wonder it's occupied by bees, you tell yourself. We step in unison ever-further off the beaten path to the foot of a wider tree. Do not overestimate your personal allowance for happiness nor underestimate your personal allowance to be forgiven, says the spirit passing through the leaves. Passed over for promotion to chief elocution officer, you joined a new militia only to find them threatening electrocution for the absence of Ts and Cs. Who wouldn't fall into a dramatic funk? A radical shift, we hear, is required to understand what it means to gain exposure to a new demographic of playfulness and power. We transcend our bodies by the contortions we put them through while making-out in broom closets during seasonal parties. You'd think occupying your own mind would be easy, but it's nothing to write home about. There's nothing in your mind about home – to write about nothing – this home – mind about.

THE NOBEL SAVAGES

This festschrift we're editing about you is full of incendiary compliments. The green trees and the yellow fields you sleep in – the roof of rain and star-cover we sleep under – remind us that our hearts once broke at your imitation of our imitation of birdsong. O noble savages that we are, we cannot say how much it means that for so long you have shared your blue jeans and lunches of edamame beans and meat soup. For your kindness now, we offer ant-eaten leaves, the return of your notebooks, and this fossil of a forefather's femur – by which you can just make out the beginnings of your own light.

OUR LAST SUPPER

The kitchen is full of knives. The trees outside are awkward in colour and movement, making the pot plant on the window-ledge above the sink look even less real. Once as sharp as the crescent moon, our conversation is softened by the candles on the table. We put on hold all we wish we didn't know about the other, and touch a big toe with a big toe. The strangers we've hired to serve dinner say, 'For dessert, may we recommend the wild beetroot and strawberry parfait.' As the blessed, there's only so much juice we can inhabit under our skin. Like nuns in the wind, our habits have gone skew-whiff. Before the night ends, we look at each other askance and spot our reflections in what's left of the cutlery, the worried spoons.

I AM NOURISHING
THE POLAR STAR AGAIN

And because I am nourishing the polar star, it is bigger and brighter than even the streetlight under which we stand – the light cast even paler than our shadows. Though this could be an allegory, it would be a poor allegory, unless you consider allegories for their distinction. In order to distinguish our shadows from the street – so grey, so tired – a passing policeman chalks our outline – which, if I may be so anti-establishment, so anti-*authoritarian*, bears me so little resemblance – the size of my head, the size of my heart –

'Heart?' you interrupt.

'Heart,' I say.

We go our separate ways forgetting that we once had a similar destination in mind, that we once performed magnificent tricks of light upon each other.

DON'T FEAR THE AUTHORITY
STARING YOU DOWN

Don't fear the authority staring you down. Say: Take your best shot. Take your hands out of your pockets, let me take your credit card out of your hand, I'll buy you a drink. We should be friends, you observe, in the reflection of the mirror-ball overhead. Which is precisely why you frighten me, not because you're a superb dancer, but because there are questions you've never even bothered to ask, such as: *Where can I send my unused train tickets for a refund?* Never underestimate the power that can come when facing an unfriendly face. Let that face lose the game you were born to lose. During times of lime green skies signalling personal as well as communal collapse, let everything, including your feelings, be captured in the neon sign advertising beer: *Cold and Cool.* Under your hair is your skull and below your skull are feelings so complex about me, who in another life is your beloved, your betrothed. There is no reason why we should stay together, you say, my beloved, my betrothed: except the party we're planning, & the house, & the dog, & the car, & the kids. Our brick-hard, door-knob dead, made-out-of-mud hearts serve us just fine as the façade for this family home. If there's a star above us, let it shine during our midnight dip in the simulated hot water springs, free of shelter, and the need to swim for shelter.

THE NEW DOCTRINE WE BRING

The children want to keep playing in the park in the rain. And who are we to say no? As their parents, we can say whatever we like it's true, but we lavish them with too much attention. Until they become so wet and so cold they want to bring the weather inside, to muck up the furniture before they muck up their futures. There are times we want to know them so much more than the person whose bed we shared in their making. From the window, we can see our beginnings beginning again: in cars, in the rain, juggling chainsaws, in a bus-shelter, drinking rosé next to a rose bush which is burning, just burning, it's still burning – in a post-coital way.

ANNO DOMINI

In this anniversary year of our *getting-it-on*, the magnitude
of our life together is even more impressive. Breathe out
our suffering, breathe in our happiness. The meaning and
purpose of harmony is only becoming known to us again,
but if we were to choose a *semblance* it would have to be
the manner by which our children are eating ice cream.
We're scooping heaps of ice cream into sugar cones, sugar
cones big as traffic cones. Out of our caution comes
longing, and out of our bowdlerization comes truth – not
so sparkly as a shower-of-stars, but sparkly nonetheless.
We triangulate on our Segways through the park until
there is no stopping us from stopping too suddenly.
Under the boughs, we hold pinecones to our chests, as if
the young of our own species.

IT WOULD TAKE A MIRACLE

Our children are starting to feel sorry for us. Why the asunder smile? Why the misguided sense of achievement? Indoors and windowless, the season never ends, though the sun by all that is holy and known by physicists and yogi should always and forever rise in the East. What miracle might we conjure to help it burn forever? To help it hover like the bright green fuzz that once grew above my lip when I was young and lonely and invincible, and you were in love and fearless and free? Dear children, tell your parents how much you enjoy hitting tennis balls at sunset, even though the sun no longer sets.

THE MOON IS SHINING
OVER THE BRIDGE

The moon is shining over the bridge, on top of the skyscraper, through the windows of this neon-lit crane. There is so much work to be done, and I am doing whatever it takes, including drugs, which speak to each other in the soft spousal way you speak to me. To make up for my transgressions – my imperfections – I invite you to take a midnight walk around the neighbourhood where we howl in unison about the infidelities of city planners. By day, I am exceedingly joyful in all my tribulations – but on nights like these, broken in spirit and limp-limbed – I'm given to unusual pleasures watching duster crop planes flying across the horizon. Every watch has an agent and every agent has to know when the time is right to pack it in, to surrender to heavier forces than even their beloved, in command of the firmament, can defend.

slips on crystal beads of light that spill like milk across the floor...

It's not so much that I want to write poems, I confess to you, as I want to not read them. There are artists who find torture in pursuit of the right word a turn-on, but the closest I've ever come to being crucified was at midnight, by candlelight, when moved to uncap a squeaking pen in the closet. The verse I wake to scribble is never worth the cookies crumbled on the bedroom carpet. And yet, once, in the back alley of a club getting stoned, we spent some quality time together. Only for you to say later how much you despised what I wrote in your name.

I AM WEARY (AND MUST REST AWHILE)

And because I am weary (and must rest awhile), allow me to lie upon your robe. I cannot rest, not upon your red and gold, not upon your blue and gold, not upon your chest that expands with each breath, not under this tree, not on this ground – the ground is *as hard*, but that is not why, the sun is *as hot*, but that is not why. Whatever the weather, whatever the *why*, I am breathing in this long breath, taking in this long month, where you have found me travelling and following the world's most popular mobile-app, swiping at your algorithm to bring us together, walking home from work / via this wood / in this changing / on this revolving / under this pneumatic… Question: when does the world around us not travel with us? When the self slips in space and time, requiring us to meet secretly in a cave in this suburban park. I am walking through the trees, I am chewing bubble gum in the clouds, I am reading what you have hashtagged on these granite walls about our continuous present, an on-going effort to complete this simple sentence, to live this not-so-simple life.

IN OUR PRESENT BODIES, WE'RE FINDING IT HARD TO MAKE IT THROUGH THE JUNGLE

It's impossible to be a part of the body politic studying like-minded primates when we can't coordinate what we see or where we step. For too long now, whenever you climbed a tree I bent over backwards, offering for landing my bad back. We do this to entertain as much as to convert. *All our bodies are holy*, we say, though your foot refuses to lend a hand, and my ear refuses to be your lookout. We tell the cannibals we live amongst to repent and make amends, but they continue to consume leg and nose, elbow and soul. If the whole body were a nose, where the seeing? If the body were a knee, where the wrist? In the past, our bodies have been hedonist and hero-playing, but today we are sluggish and prone to cramping – the feet that chase our feet have run marathons… and so we learn to live with phantom pain.

ALPHA AND OMEGA

Our witness of life's mysteries is finally beginning to pay dividends. A, with the big brain and the hopeful soul, says there's not so much separating us from the peach pie in the window. We take what we want. We want what we need. One lesson we might take from such an analogy is: if we allow for signs of divinity (and/or alien abduction) the superhuman need to understand our beginnings will someday be met – like when a body from the bottom of the ocean rises to meet a body falling from the heights of the sky. A's lover, Z – with the heavy heart and the ambivalent orgasms – prefers the tang of endings to the sprite of beginnings. Clearing my diary when I'm both rising and falling out of bed is about confidence as much as it's about being a master of time. *There is a leaf stain on your chin*, I write, *dear A. And a sky stain on yours, dear Z.* PS: all time leads to this: a desire to taste the collapsing of sweet space. PSS: there is nothing sweeter than sweet space. PSSS: unless you consider these lines sweet. *Sweet sweet.*

A NEW GHOST IS AMONG US

A new ghost is among us. We head South with the sun to study how the soul responds to massage and fresh fruit bat curry. We drink sex-on-the-beach then have sex on the beach with the aim of becoming depression proof. We may not become depression proof, but our new ghost becomes depression proof. We tune in, turn on, and drop out of our regular lives for longer than the longest stretch of beach. And now the water is as warm as the mouth that we're kissing. We lose the medallion with the emblazoned image of the old ghost that came before the new ghost, who was so super-sensitive to our feelings. And so, we dive down into these old depths, where we find not our medallion but that old ghost: winding through the reef, between our legs, around our heads, reminding us of our dull faculties and the radiance that we might find even when short of air and sky.

WE'RE TRYING TO YOKE
THIS YOKELESS BULL

In this land of barley-eaters, in this corn-land, the clay is red, and the red is gold and the scrub-brush clings to the hill where the bull roots and tufts. From the sky comes rain and with the rain ruin, and those of us singing this hymn slip in pursuit of a word that's untranslatable. The bull flicks and huffs his hoof, looking more and more fierce, despite our threat of castration, our threat of butchery. It is always a child in such stories who whispers word after word into the bull's ear: eyes of butter, mouth of flour. Upon this hillside of fallen sky, whatever word would save a bull's life, we don't know it. Even after we hear it.

I AM NO PROPHET

I can't tell you what's sweeping through these country fields, except these runaway horses. Sweeping through these fields, according to the data… I mean, sleeping through the Sabbath, according to this magazine on animal husbandry, is not at all unusual for the world we're living in. Up the last rung of the ladder, we're fixing shingles broken by a horse last seen twerking in the direction of passers-by. Under the radar – hidden in the low-level ranches of these dust-brown fields / white-clouds / blue-skies – we find these hours we're uninsured the greatest risk of our lives. *The horses aren't just bucking*, someone says, *they're remembering*. And when we hear this, we're reminded of ourselves riding high. Albeit without sunglasses, the kind that make us look like cowboys, even though we've long walked away from the farm – long walked away from the cows.

ON THE HILLSIDE, WITH SHEEP...

wandering without intention, knocking wet wool with dingle-berries, rubbing lankness against barbed wire and the gatepost's hinge. Between this land and the neighbours there is a long, frost-riddled fence, ignored for the free roaming of red and blue, spray-dotted wool. If there is a matriarch amongst us, she will understand it is not grazing nor sheering time. When the cars pull up, know that not all doorways are meant to be entered. Run to hide in the scrub-brush and scree: away from the rolled-down windows and shutters of cameras, the exclamations of parents and the extended arms of children, who will forever chase you across the earth away from these idylls of curb.

OUR COLLECTIVE POSSIBILITY

Our collective possibility fills us with promise. Those who acquire manners young are gracious, but those who are gracious don't necessarily acquire manners young, so we are told by the woman selling flowers at the restaurant. Sitting next to us at the bar, we underestimate the great strength of the nose-bleeders who beat us game after game in a befallen softball league for local businesses. If only we could be redeemed by our children, who play their music too loud and sleep with each other in the woods underneath the night stars. Stoically, we leave it up to the bulls we run with to decide whether to skewer us or trample us.

THERE'S HOPE THAT
ANYTHING IS POSSIBLE

There's hope that anything is possible. The sun sets in one world and rises over the next, glamorous and distant and impossible to simulate in even the best theme parks, where the roller coasters carry you upside down and the lights flash as a mirror of the sky in the sea. Against the advice of church and state, we burn pink marshmallows black & blue over the BBQ we've found smouldering in the rain. Our journey toward this other side of living will always be just this side of knowable. We look to the glowing screens of our phones, where we can see on the horizon something vying with the weather, the same which we carry in our knees as pain.

TOMBSTONING

The teenagers scream for ice cream from ice cream vans, before they turn to eat each other: like the crabs in rock faces that slide into the sea – only more romantically – like the crabs in neon colours from the marine aquarium down the street. With their confabulations and strange grouping of consonances, our small sea-side town turns its head to watch them inch towards the cliff's edge before they step into the air, straight-backed as tombstones to sputter into the blue-black of the Sound, where Napoleon was once imprisoned on an HMS, and the local millionaire is regularly refused planning to turn an island of former MoD barracks into a 5-star resort. They don't care about the passenger ferry that can take you to France. Occasionally, one of them breaks a neck, but the splash lights up the ocean as if the night sky.

I AM GONE TO WHERE
NO ONE HAS GONE BEFORE

Let the truths and rules of order that have been laid down be your teacher. No one less than me likes the odds of last year's returning champs returning again. *Âvuso*, someone might say, but this title is more suited for a younger brother than a venerable elder. You may only be a stream-winner but the story of your uplift to *nibbāna* will be legendary amongst jet-setters someday. Who above you, you'd be right to ask, deserves to be treated as if they are above you? With no spots-of-time to be recollected in our periphery, there's a level playing field of space and a spreading osmosis of tranquillity captured. In this world of speeding mopeds, who are we to argue with a noise that lingers longer than the speed of light? The smoke never dissipates into the dusky sky but stays with us, obscuring the view from our lungs. It is possible that light from the clouds will speak to us if we play the violin. But neither of us have ever played the violin, whose dark body is more readily held & hunched over than our own.

THE NEW LANGUAGE WE'RE SPEAKING

The new language we're speaking sounds like cheering from the side-lines when – WHAM! – right in front of us the cornerback is hit. We watch his soul float high in the sky, to mingle with the cheerleaders in the clouds. We count our lost blessings on fingers held up in the name of getting all the Wolverines who've fallen back in the game. When it's over, we drive our 4x4s across town to slurp Cokes and eat hamburgers to build stamina. The moon lingers fizzingly on our lips and the wind plays number games with our minds. We've suffered so much loss this season, we should by now be accustomed to licking our collective wounds. Still, we reach for our bullhorns, our megaphones, our speaking trumpets and ask, in all the tongues we know, the reason for our destruction.

THROUGH THE WOODS,
WE'RE RUNNING WITH THE LIGHT

Through the woods, we're running with the light. Our feet barely touch the sticks and leaves covering the ground. *Where are we going?* you ask me, as the trees fall around us. And though I don't know, I pretend to know. And you follow me, as so many have followed me before, until we wind up back here, at the Waffle House. And soon it is 3 a.m., and the storm has gotten stronger, but the coffee is still hot, and the waiter is still smiling, and the waffles are still sweet. There are more celebrated men in the history of this world than me, but do they sing any better of the reasons we return to this house of late-night dwellers? The testimony of this booth-enhanced space is something we're forced to leave before the answer comes, again and again.

IN THE NAME OF THE FATHER

The moonlight follows us into the bedroom, rich with tapestries and peacock feathers. My 70th son has an earache which keeps him and me and his 69 brothers awake at night. If you ask me about the moon, I'll tell you that I loved and was loved. Not accounting for the pleasures of variance, the number of wives I've had is speculated to be as high as 36 (deduced by Shechem) and as low as 6 (calculated by Abimelech). I could tell you of your place, above all the others, under my sheets, but tonight I cannot help but wonder if I might conceive and carry a 71st child, a daughter, myself.

THE ORTHODONTISTS

The orthodontists are sailing out of town. Our children no longer recline in white offices with white office chairs, mouths propped open to the dangers of apples, a halo glowing in their eyes from the light overhead. Standing on the train tracks on the train's bridge we watch as they wade into the river until a fisherman, at our bidding, casts a hand-tied fly and pulls a child by her metalwork through the air, stopping her from swimming upstream and away from us and our nostalgia for nitrous and Novocaine.

MY GHOST HOVERS OVER ME

Walking through the park of this seaside village: *Ghost*, I say, *take this plastic take-away tub of chirashi, help me scatter the rice from the imperfect ends of sushi rolls as an offering for your pain and suffering.* Together, my ghost and I walk barefoot over the grass, foraging for mushrooms and spring onions. Dark clouds obscure the brown ground. Not all litanies end with hope, my ghost, but here and now don't blame me for your untimely demise, and I won't misrepresent you for the miasma which brought the cholera and now the chlamydia to our seaside village of moveable feasts.

I AM NOT WORTHY THAT THOU SHOULD'ST COME UNDER MY ROOF

And because I am not worthy that thou should'st come under my roof, my manifestoes are performing themselves:

Manifesto 1: Slink out of the house…

Manifesto 2: Through the back door…

Manifesto 3: The door might be a window…

Manifesto 4: Out of which I climb to hide in the poolside cabana until you are gone.

A 5th unwritten Manifesto about how I might become worthy is dispelled like smoke from a *J* and fills the air of the cabana, where there is: a defunct BBQ, an empty 2 and ½ gallon gas canister, a croquet set with a single mallet, a broken lawnmower, a pool skimmer with dead dragonflies, an inflatable octopus… several low-slung, reclinable chairs.

Many years pass like this – with you in the house and me in the cabana… neither of us availing of the cool blue waters that shimmer in the deep Earth that lies between us.

WE'RE DRIVING NORTH

We're driving north in our little red car to a little red *stuga*. My glass of mineral water splashing over the dash smells of sweat and sea-salt, detergent and fortitude. To be incarnate not as a victim of our own country, but as one who charts the evolution of distressed, pale floorboards barely requires the voice of a visa-granting authority. There's no need to denounce or deport us... we would have gladly taken the gun-shot that took the life of your beloved King at the masked ball. With no more seats in the drawing room, we're careening to sit on the nearest lap. We'd trade our bodies for your mountains and our minds for your rivers that flood the valley with fjords.

I AM SO HAPPY, I SAID (PART 1)

I am so happy, I said, as I watched you jumping rope, I could jump right out of my office chair and into that space which is joy. I wanted to say, *into outside*, but joy doesn't need to reside outside, not when there's so much joy inside on the Xbox. Our children often jump for no reason, as if jumping is more than an expression of joy, it *brings* joy. Like the famous poet once said: *Jumping from reading to writing is the greatest joy of my life*. What a life! But just as fast I say this, neither my life nor this metaphor are 100% working for me anymore. The idea of jumping is already posing questions I can't answer. Despite everything, our future could still be rosy, if only the roses could find a way to rise up the lattice against the rainy Spring. We want more live music, more margaritas, more shared experiences with the hand-held wand massager, more TV series about couples like us who are ready to experiment with Alpine skiing, bigger bathroom sinks, and camping parties with their most spiritually-liberated friends. To find again the source of the Kool-Aid which used to flow freely from the garden fountain is to enter a poem like this – so full of truth in its fictions and as close as we'll ever get to God. It brings back the pain in our knees suffered from jumping off a minor mogul last winter: YELP! Why jump, you may ask yourself, when joy could be expressed so many other ways without incurring pain? Singing like I am, I'm minded to ask: when was the last time you sang? The relationship between poetry and song I've thought too much about, it's true, and yet I've never really sung anything this joyful. To sing, in my mind, is to suffer, and so to scream: AAAAARRRRGGGGHHHH!, as the famous poet screamed while hanging our new pendulum light over the dining table when I accidentally switched on the mains. The only real way to express joy, I've long thought, is to write hard into the night. But just as quickly as I say this, sitting here now, in this dark, in this silence, I'm not feeling the initial joy with which I began writing. What if this poem isn't such a joyous poem after all? What's there to be joyful about in this world of so much grief and so few poems about the wonder of all we don't know: about each other and our beginnings, our longings and our long, slow demise... who knows what comes next?! It's been so long since I've asked any real questions, with a popsicle in my mouth, the sort that melts as you're journeying from insouciance to experience in a poem of two parts.

I AM SO HAPPY, I SAID (PART 2)

Though, now that I hear myself saying this, I wonder if I may have prematurely propelled this poem into a complicated space, replacing Romantic conceptions of the sublime with postmodern ideas about our displacement of fear and awe in favour of accepting a manageable (and so *prescribeable*) low-level, smiling emoji of anxiety. *Who,* I hear you saying to me when you wake in the morning from uneasy dreams, *even has time to write emails about the sublime anymore!?* I ask this question of our psycho-therapist who emails to tell me that a) I deserve to be alone, and b) that you and she are running off together to make love every day in the warm corners of the globe ☺. On my own, I go to the art house cinema, Starbucks, grocery shopping, do the laundry. Sometimes, when one's metaphysical socks and underwear don't make it to the hamper, there's little joy in the bedroom. This – if you think like the whole world does, and I DO – shouldn't mean we're all doomed, but it DOES. *Meta-physicality,* never mind *masculinity,* is in crisis, which may be why it's been the subject of so many of my recent poems… all of which I *hate!* This poem was supposed to be my amazing grace. Instead of Joy, I was going to call this poem *Grace,* but there's nothing graceful about punching a keyboard as if you want to beat it to death. Even if it's a wireless Apple keyboard, like this one, made of cool white keys and some sort of steel that's probably been invented by NASA. This may be becoming the easiest second part to a poem I've ever written; which is another way of saying, it's never going to reach enlightenment. So many of my recent poems require so much research, nobody in their right mind would read them. It's possible that nobody wants to read them because they *lack* research, and so that certain *je ne sais quoi* that comes when the mind is really firing beyond its own synapses. What I've been calling *research,* of course, is really just living, sometimes badly, sometimes with my head full of dung, or in the clouds, not seeing what's really happening, but being surprised enough to smile when the shitty things I've thought wouldn't come true come true ☺. *So cynical!* You've been a good friend, I want to write to you now: in the form of my wife, my boyfriend, my reader, my *nobody*. You can finish this poem for me. I will be just over here, where I am most days, preparing to sleep in the reclining chair in the corner of my office. If I wake before you're finished, I will return to our world again, thinking about words and long poems and how, even when we don't care for them, they've always cared for us.

I AM LIGHT THREEFOLD, MEASURER OF THE REGION, EXHAUSTLESS HEAT, BURNT-OBLATION

And because I am light three-fold, measurer of the region, exhaustless heat, burnt-oblation, the villagers have come out of the forest to hang blessings around my neck. The experience of being blessed comes as a paradoxical event after a day spent picking fruit under blistering sun on a reality TV show featuring extended family, former lovers, co-workers, the newly enlightened and carefree. Inconspicuously absent are the plagues, famines, and war, as the saying goes, that have been a constant in this part of the world since day nought. All of us – contestants that we are – have the same unique opportunity to be coeval with the deepest part of the sky, and yet how rarely we choose to be coeval with the deepest part of the sky. In time, we're confident we'll understand light from light, bluebird from bluebird, green vines from green vines, swinging. But this region, we hear, will soon be under water, and those of us with fire in our hands are wary of water.

THE RIVER FLOWS OVER ME / OVERFLOWS ME

The river flows over me / overflows me. There are so many people in the river / so many rivers in the people. If I ever get the time and space to study the river, I'll ask you to make love with me in the river. So many children we'll have, we'll make them eat breakfast. So many bananas we'll peel, to thunk from the edge of their spoons into their Cheerios, into the river. A person throws a ball into the river. A dog dives after the ball. Another person dives after the dog… and soon all are drowning in the river. A promising photographer looks into the river and starts snapping pictures. There are so many bottles in the river. The photographer's camera is fast. But this poem – floating like a ship in a bottle down the river – is faster.

NO EUPHEMISM CAN PREVENT THE
RAIN FROM COMING BETWEEN US

No euphemism can prevent the rain from coming between us. Between the two of us, we no longer need a map to get the kids to school. We know it like the back of the other's hand as it reaches for coffee in the morning. Despite the microbeads of plastic in the water, the benefits of living here are considerably more than the benefits of living elsewhere – e.g. our sushi's seaweed is sustainable and tastes of the sun. We drive steadily outward from the centre, perpetuating the study of po-ethics and an appreciation for plotted green spaces. Our misunderstanding of time and its keeping means we're late for pick-up again. We mop our brows with towels that smell of pepperoni or peppermint, we can't tell which. At the dinner table, we sit as a family, holding correctly our forks and throwing food.

OUR FEELINGS DEMAND
AN INTERVENTION

Our feelings demand an intervention. There's low-level self-righteousness in the air. We're rewriting the past in the words of prophets promising a happy hereafter. On the front porch, our eponymous protagonist is granted his future in-laws' approval, despite the fact that their daughter is already *sans* underwear and sporting a demonic appetite for brains. Too much sex and too many drugs means we're slipping out of apocrypha and into a true tale of *enfants terribles*. Against the current trend of good intentions, we overturn the smorgasbord that's been set by the marketing department and begin an almighty food fight in the garden. From the balcony, we watch an improvised performance of recrimination by the same characters whose souls we sold to the highest bidder. Above us, the gods have never been so necessary.

WALKING DOWN HYACINTH, ON THE WAY TO BOUGAINVILLEA

Walking down Hyacinth, on the way to Bougainvillea, already it's night and your parents have the kids. The handbag you bought today is the dusky colour of vomit after too much red wine, but you refuse to let it phase you. The sun is bright and the houses – pink, green and white – overlook the beach where our little boy complained of a rash on his chest and sore nipples. We'll rub some cream on it when we get home, you said. Whipped cream, he said? Which is what your mother promised him on his ice cream tonight. On Asphodel, we buy some strawberry-banana from The Popcorn Shop. Together, we are gearing up to do something worthy of exaltation. And it is still only Wednesday, the day before Christmas.

THESE FLOWERS CONCERN ME

These flowers concern me. Not because they're not beautiful, but because they're so beautiful they're starting to smell like the human body after three weeks underground, in all its funk. To be subterranean, even for a little while, is a worry, especially for those of us who refuse to worry. And so we move from the retiring heat to the frozen terra, where each glacier is challenged by the spikes of hot springs that provide geo-thermal energy. In this coldest part of the world, who would've expected green-houses of papaya and passion fruit to testify to new life? *The after-party is always better than the party*, our host tells us, before handing us freshly-blended drinks, in which we soon float clinging to ice cubes like rafts amidst plastic umbrellas.

I AM MEEK AND LOWLY AT HEART

A liberation of mind is suffusing. We rejoice over the yellow leaves falling from the sky, piled six feet high. We scare the neighbours by jumping out of trees into the leaves with our rakes raised. We're on our way home from work, when we stop to buy a beer and cheeseburger. We could be heroes, if we could just hold each other's thoughts in our heads for the duration of our walk. For so long now, we've been heading for this point of departure, away from the downtown parade we've stopped to watch. When the authorities finally appear on horseback, we're not disappointed by the intervention. To those standing in front – with your gigantic heads and heavy balloons – we ask that you lower your heads, that you let fly your balloons.

THERE'S TALK OF A SECOND ASSASSINATION ATTEMPT

Of one of us. By the other. The details are hazy. We assume the worst of each other, but disguise this with offers of togetherness: *I'll share the chateaubriand, if you share the watermelon sorbet; I'll share the sunrises if you compel me the sunsets.* Our greatest virtue, beyond the power that comes with patience, is our knowledge of providential failure, and the hope that we'll be forgiven for buckling at the knees when we're called home to betray the other. Threats of injury and persecution affect us in roundabout ways. We fear both glory and deceit, commendation and nothingness. A failed paradox sets in when we discover one of us was meant for divine intervention... but which one? Weakness was never really our strength. We rise and fall through the other's eyes until we're held like a new sin. The rewards that were meant to someday be ours will be received by heartier losers than us.

I AM WITH YOU ALWAYS, EVEN UNTO
THE END OF THE WORLD

And because I am with you always, even unto the end
of the world, you look concerned. To spend one lifetime
together is forgivable, but *two* is lazy. It's a sign of the
times that everyone, everywhere, is disappointed with
the results of our ongoing mission for transcendence.
Our resolve to know if we'll make it to the end of the
movie we're watching confirms devotion does not come
without doubt. A sign of a really good movie is wanting
a different ending when we already know the ending. At
dinner, we're reminded that we are the reason endings gets
written slowly, word by word, scene by scene. We plan to
stay awake until bed, where we'll perform with just the
right amount of duty and neglect. But already we're tired,
from the meaning we've been making all of our lives – we
blow meaning away with the candlelight, pull it away with
the tablecloth: leaving behind the table (flickering), the
TV (flickering), you and me (flickering away).

DOWN IN OUR GRAVES

Now that we are down in our graves, this end-game we're playing has me re-thinking transgressions. If we can forget about betrayal (of us / of the divine / of the divine in us) – if we can forget about why (why?) – we'll remember that togetherness comes when the electrical impulse of life is plugged into what's possible after burial. There's a crunching sound like chocolate-covered ants marching over each other between our teeth, bringing us back to the surface of the Earth, like a little death without the sticky pleasantness. The taste may be wholly of home, but the sensation is of the darkness that comes when you encounter lost space. Looking up at the night sky, we see the path we're carving between this life and the next could easily be extinguished by anyone with the right rocket. In a time of lost consciousness, we take turns vacillating between ill tidings and unknown joy each time one of us, like a long-forgotten God, rises from the dead.

NOTE

'The most beautiful thing we can experience is the mysterious… To know what is impenetrable to us really exists, manifesting itself as the highest wisdom and the most radiant beauty, which our dull faculties can comprehend only in their most primitive forms, this knowledge, this feeling is at the centre of true religiousness' (Albert Einstein). Nothwithstanding, there are allusions throughout to the Bible, the Qur'an, & the Buddhist Sutras. Notwithstanding, notwithstanding, the angel with the speaking trumpet in the middle of the disco ball on the cover is a detail from *The Last Judgement* by Joos van Cleve.

Lightning Source UK Ltd.
Milton Keynes UK
UKHW041046010319

338103UK00001B/52/P